I0765904

Bon Apetit!

Ultimate Personal and Family Meal Planning Diary

@ Journals & Notebooks

Copyright 2016

All Rights reserved. No part of this book may be reproduced or used in any way or formor by any means whether electronic or mechanical, this means that you cannot recordor photocopy any material ideas or tips that are provided in this book.

MONDAY	TUESDAY	WEDNESDAY	THURSDAY

GROCERIES

FRIDAY	SATURDAY	SUNDAY	NOTES

GROCERIES

RECIPES

MONDAY	TUESDAY	WEDNESDAY	THURSDAY

GROCERIES

FRIDAY	SATURDAY	SUNDAY	NOTES

GROCERIES

RECIPES

MONDAY	TUESDAY	WEDNESDAY	THURSDAY

GROCERIES

FRIDAY	SATURDAY	SUNDAY	NOTES

GROCERIES

RECIPES

MONDAY	TUESDAY	WEDNESDAY	THURSDAY

GROCERIES

FRIDAY	SATURDAY	SUNDAY	NOTES

GROCERIES

RECIPES

MONDAY	TUESDAY	WEDNESDAY	THURSDAY

GROCERIES

FRIDAY	SATURDAY	SUNDAY	NOTES

GROCERIES

RECIPES

MONDAY	TUESDAY	WEDNESDAY	THURSDAY

FRIDAY	SATURDAY	SUNDAY	NOTES

<table>
<tr><td>MONDAY</td><td>TUESDAY</td><td>WEDNESDAY</td><td>THURSDAY</td></tr>
</table>

GROCERIES

<table>
<tr><td>FRIDAY</td><td>SATURDAY</td><td>SUNDAY</td><td>NOTES</td></tr>
</table>

GROCERIES

RECIPES

MONDAY	TUESDAY	WEDNESDAY	THURSDAY

GROCERIES

FRIDAY	SATURDAY	SUNDAY	NOTES

GROCERIES

RECIPES

<table>
<tr><td>MONDAY</td><td>TUESDAY</td><td>WEDNESDAY</td><td>THURSDAY</td></tr>
</table>

GROCERIES

<table>
<tr><td>FRIDAY</td><td>SATURDAY</td><td>SUNDAY</td><td>NOTES</td></tr>
</table>

GROCERIES

RECIPES

MONDAY	TUESDAY	WEDNESDAY	THURSDAY

GROCERIES

FRIDAY	SATURDAY	SUNDAY	NOTES

GROCERIES

RECIPES

MONDAY	TUESDAY	WEDNESDAY	THURSDAY

GROCERIES

FRIDAY	SATURDAY	SUNDAY	NOTES

GROCERIES

RECIPES

MONDAY	TUESDAY	WEDNESDAY	THURSDAY

GROCERIES

FRIDAY	SATURDAY	SUNDAY	NOTES

GROCERIES

RECIPES

MONDAY	TUESDAY	WEDNESDAY	THURSDAY

GROCERIES

FRIDAY	SATURDAY	SUNDAY	NOTES

GROCERIES

RECIPES

MONDAY	TUESDAY	WEDNESDAY	THURSDAY

GROCERIES

FRIDAY	SATURDAY	SUNDAY	NOTES

GROCERIES

RECIPES

MONDAY	TUESDAY	WEDNESDAY	THURSDAY

GROCERIES

FRIDAY	SATURDAY	SUNDAY	NOTES

GROCERIES

RECIPES

MONDAY	TUESDAY	WEDNESDAY	THURSDAY

GROCERIES

FRIDAY	SATURDAY	SUNDAY	NOTES

GROCERIES

RECIPES

MONDAY	TUESDAY	WEDNESDAY	THURSDAY

GROCERIES

FRIDAY	SATURDAY	SUNDAY	NOTES

GROCERIES

RECIPES

MONDAY	TUESDAY	WEDNESDAY	THURSDAY

GROCERIES

FRIDAY	SATURDAY	SUNDAY	NOTES

GROCERIES

RECIPES

MONDAY	TUESDAY	WEDNESDAY	THURSDAY

GROCERIES

FRIDAY	SATURDAY	SUNDAY	NOTES

GROCERIES

RECIPES

MONDAY	TUESDAY	WEDNESDAY	THURSDAY

GROCERIES

FRIDAY	SATURDAY	SUNDAY	NOTES

GROCERIES

RECIPES

MONDAY	TUESDAY	WEDNESDAY	THURSDAY

GROCERIES

FRIDAY	SATURDAY	SUNDAY	NOTES

GROCERIES

RECIPES

MONDAY	TUESDAY	WEDNESDAY	THURSDAY

FRIDAY	SATURDAY	SUNDAY	NOTES

MONDAY	TUESDAY	WEDNESDAY	THURSDAY

GROCERIES

FRIDAY	SATURDAY	SUNDAY	NOTES

GROCERIES

RECIPES

MONDAY	TUESDAY	WEDNESDAY	THURSDAY

GROCERIES

FRIDAY	SATURDAY	SUNDAY	NOTES

GROCERIES

RECIPES

MONDAY	TUESDAY	WEDNESDAY	THURSDAY

GROCERIES

FRIDAY	SATURDAY	SUNDAY	NOTES

GROCERIES

RECIPES

MONDAY	TUESDAY	WEDNESDAY	THURSDAY

GROCERIES

FRIDAY	SATURDAY	SUNDAY	NOTES

GROCERIES

RECIPES

MONDAY	TUESDAY	WEDNESDAY	THURSDAY

GROCERIES

FRIDAY	SATURDAY	SUNDAY	NOTES

GROCERIES

RECIPES

MONDAY	TUESDAY	WEDNESDAY	THURSDAY

GROCERIES

FRIDAY	SATURDAY	SUNDAY	NOTES

GROCERIES

RECIPES

MONDAY	TUESDAY	WEDNESDAY	THURSDAY

GROCERIES

FRIDAY	SATURDAY	SUNDAY	NOTES

GROCERIES

RECIPES

MONDAY	TUESDAY	WEDNESDAY	THURSDAY

GROCERIES

FRIDAY	SATURDAY	SUNDAY	NOTES

GROCERIES

RECIPES

MONDAY	TUESDAY	WEDNESDAY	THURSDAY

FRIDAY	SATURDAY	SUNDAY	NOTES

MONDAY	TUESDAY	WEDNESDAY	THURSDAY

GROCERIES

FRIDAY	SATURDAY	SUNDAY	NOTES

GROCERIES

RECIPES

MONDAY	TUESDAY	WEDNESDAY	THURSDAY

GROCERIES

FRIDAY	SATURDAY	SUNDAY	NOTES

GROCERIES

RECIPES

MONDAY	TUESDAY	WEDNESDAY	THURSDAY

GROCERIES

FRIDAY	SATURDAY	SUNDAY	NOTES

GROCERIES

RECIPES

MONDAY	TUESDAY	WEDNESDAY	THURSDAY

GROCERIES

FRIDAY	SATURDAY	SUNDAY	NOTES

GROCERIES

RECIPES

MONDAY	TUESDAY	WEDNESDAY	THURSDAY

GROCERIES

FRIDAY	SATURDAY	SUNDAY	NOTES

GROCERIES

RECIPES

MONDAY	TUESDAY	WEDNESDAY	THURSDAY

GROCERIES

FRIDAY	SATURDAY	SUNDAY	NOTES

GROCERIES

RECIPES

MONDAY	TUESDAY	WEDNESDAY	THURSDAY

GROCERIES

FRIDAY	SATURDAY	SUNDAY	NOTES

GROCERIES

RECIPES

MONDAY	TUESDAY	WEDNESDAY	THURSDAY

GROCERIES

FRIDAY	SATURDAY	SUNDAY	NOTES

GROCERIES

RECIPES

MONDAY	TUESDAY	WEDNESDAY	THURSDAY

GROCERIES

FRIDAY	SATURDAY	SUNDAY	NOTES

GROCERIES

RECIPES

MONDAY	TUESDAY	WEDNESDAY	THURSDAY

GROCERIES

FRIDAY	SATURDAY	SUNDAY	NOTES

GROCERIES

RECIPES

MONDAY	TUESDAY	WEDNESDAY	THURSDAY

GROCERIES

FRIDAY	SATURDAY	SUNDAY	NOTES

GROCERIES

RECIPES

MONDAY	TUESDAY	WEDNESDAY	THURSDAY

GROCERIES

FRIDAY	SATURDAY	SUNDAY	NOTES

GROCERIES

RECIPES

MONDAY	TUESDAY	WEDNESDAY	THURSDAY

GROCERIES

FRIDAY	SATURDAY	SUNDAY	NOTES

GROCERIES

RECIPES

MONDAY	TUESDAY	WEDNESDAY	THURSDAY

GROCERIES

FRIDAY	SATURDAY	SUNDAY	NOTES

GROCERIES

RECIPES

MONDAY	TUESDAY	WEDNESDAY	THURSDAY

FRIDAY	SATURDAY	SUNDAY	NOTES

MONDAY	TUESDAY	WEDNESDAY	THURSDAY

GROCERIES

FRIDAY	SATURDAY	SUNDAY	NOTES

GROCERIES

RECIPES

MONDAY	TUESDAY	WEDNESDAY	THURSDAY

GROCERIES

FRIDAY	SATURDAY	SUNDAY	NOTES

GROCERIES

RECIPES

MONDAY	TUESDAY	WEDNESDAY	THURSDAY

GROCERIES

FRIDAY	SATURDAY	SUNDAY	NOTES

GROCERIES

RECIPES

MONDAY	TUESDAY	WEDNESDAY	THURSDAY

GROCERIES

FRIDAY	SATURDAY	SUNDAY	NOTES

GROCERIES

RECIPES

MONDAY	TUESDAY	WEDNESDAY	THURSDAY

GROCERIES

FRIDAY	SATURDAY	SUNDAY	NOTES

GROCERIES

RECIPES

MONDAY	TUESDAY	WEDNESDAY	THURSDAY

GROCERIES

FRIDAY	SATURDAY	SUNDAY	NOTES

GROCERIES

RECIPES

MONDAY	TUESDAY	WEDNESDAY	THURSDAY

GROCERIES

FRIDAY	SATURDAY	SUNDAY	NOTES

GROCERIES

RECIPES

MONDAY	TUESDAY	WEDNESDAY	THURSDAY

FRIDAY	SATURDAY	SUNDAY	NOTES

MONDAY	TUESDAY	WEDNESDAY	THURSDAY

GROCERIES

FRIDAY	SATURDAY	SUNDAY	NOTES

GROCERIES

RECIPES

MONDAY	TUESDAY	WEDNESDAY	THURSDAY

GROCERIES

FRIDAY	SATURDAY	SUNDAY	NOTES

GROCERIES

RECIPES

MONDAY	TUESDAY	WEDNESDAY	THURSDAY

GROCERIES

FRIDAY	SATURDAY	SUNDAY	NOTES

GROCERIES

RECIPES

MONDAY	TUESDAY	WEDNESDAY	THURSDAY

GROCERIES

FRIDAY	SATURDAY	SUNDAY	NOTES

GROCERIES

RECIPES

MONDAY	TUESDAY	WEDNESDAY	THURSDAY

GROCERIES

FRIDAY	SATURDAY	SUNDAY	NOTES

GROCERIES

RECIPES

MONDAY	TUESDAY	WEDNESDAY	THURSDAY

GROCERIES

FRIDAY	SATURDAY	SUNDAY	NOTES

GROCERIES

RECIPES

MONDAY	TUESDAY	WEDNESDAY	THURSDAY

GROCERIES

FRIDAY	SATURDAY	SUNDAY	NOTES

GROCERIES

RECIPES

MONDAY	TUESDAY	WEDNESDAY	THURSDAY

GROCERIES

FRIDAY	SATURDAY	SUNDAY	NOTES

GROCERIES

RECIPES

MONDAY	TUESDAY	WEDNESDAY	THURSDAY

GROCERIES

FRIDAY	SATURDAY	SUNDAY	NOTES

GROCERIES

RECIPES

MONDAY	TUESDAY	WEDNESDAY	THURSDAY

GROCERIES

FRIDAY	SATURDAY	SUNDAY	NOTES

GROCERIES

RECIPES

MONDAY	TUESDAY	WEDNESDAY	THURSDAY

GROCERIES

FRIDAY	SATURDAY	SUNDAY	NOTES

GROCERIES

RECIPES

MONDAY	TUESDAY	WEDNESDAY	THURSDAY

FRIDAY	SATURDAY	SUNDAY	NOTES

MONDAY	TUESDAY	WEDNESDAY	THURSDAY

GROCERIES

FRIDAY	SATURDAY	SUNDAY	NOTES

GROCERIES

RECIPES

MONDAY	TUESDAY	WEDNESDAY	THURSDAY

GROCERIES

FRIDAY	SATURDAY	SUNDAY	NOTES

GROCERIES

RECIPES

MONDAY	TUESDAY	WEDNESDAY	THURSDAY

GROCERIES

FRIDAY	SATURDAY	SUNDAY	NOTES

GROCERIES

RECIPES

MONDAY	TUESDAY	WEDNESDAY	THURSDAY

GROCERIES

FRIDAY	SATURDAY	SUNDAY	NOTES

GROCERIES

RECIPES

MONDAY	TUESDAY	WEDNESDAY	THURSDAY

GROCERIES

FRIDAY	SATURDAY	SUNDAY	NOTES

GROCERIES

RECIPES

MONDAY	TUESDAY	WEDNESDAY	THURSDAY

GROCERIES

FRIDAY	SATURDAY	SUNDAY	NOTES

GROCERIES

RECIPES

MONDAY	TUESDAY	WEDNESDAY	THURSDAY

GROCERIES

FRIDAY	SATURDAY	SUNDAY	NOTES

GROCERIES

RECIPES

MONDAY	TUESDAY	WEDNESDAY	THURSDAY

GROCERIES

FRIDAY	SATURDAY	SUNDAY	NOTES

GROCERIES

RECIPES

MONDAY	TUESDAY	WEDNESDAY	THURSDAY

GROCERIES

FRIDAY	SATURDAY	SUNDAY	NOTES

GROCERIES

RECIPES

MONDAY	TUESDAY	WEDNESDAY	THURSDAY

GROCERIES

FRIDAY	SATURDAY	SUNDAY	NOTES

GROCERIES

RECIPES

MONDAY	TUESDAY	WEDNESDAY	THURSDAY

GROCERIES

FRIDAY	SATURDAY	SUNDAY	NOTES

GROCERIES

RECIPES

MONDAY	TUESDAY	WEDNESDAY	THURSDAY

GROCERIES

FRIDAY	SATURDAY	SUNDAY	NOTES

GROCERIES

RECIPES

MONDAY	TUESDAY	WEDNESDAY	THURSDAY

GROCERIES

FRIDAY	SATURDAY	SUNDAY	NOTES

GROCERIES

RECIPES

MONDAY	TUESDAY	WEDNESDAY	THURSDAY

GROCERIES

FRIDAY	SATURDAY	SUNDAY	NOTES

GROCERIES

RECIPES

MONDAY	TUESDAY	WEDNESDAY	THURSDAY

GROCERIES

FRIDAY	SATURDAY	SUNDAY	NOTES

GROCERIES

RECIPES

MONDAY	TUESDAY	WEDNESDAY	THURSDAY

GROCERIES

FRIDAY	SATURDAY	SUNDAY	NOTES

GROCERIES

RECIPES

MONDAY	TUESDAY	WEDNESDAY	THURSDAY

GROCERIES

FRIDAY	SATURDAY	SUNDAY	NOTES

GROCERIES

RECIPES

MONDAY	TUESDAY	WEDNESDAY	THURSDAY

GROCERIES

FRIDAY	SATURDAY	SUNDAY	NOTES

GROCERIES

RECIPES

MONDAY	TUESDAY	WEDNESDAY	THURSDAY

GROCERIES

FRIDAY	SATURDAY	SUNDAY	NOTES

GROCERIES

RECIPES

MONDAY	TUESDAY	WEDNESDAY	THURSDAY

GROCERIES

FRIDAY	SATURDAY	SUNDAY	NOTES

GROCERIES

RECIPES

MONDAY	TUESDAY	WEDNESDAY	THURSDAY

GROCERIES

FRIDAY	SATURDAY	SUNDAY	NOTES

GROCERIES

RECIPES

MONDAY	TUESDAY	WEDNESDAY	THURSDAY

GROCERIES

FRIDAY	SATURDAY	SUNDAY	NOTES

GROCERIES

RECIPES

MONDAY	TUESDAY	WEDNESDAY	THURSDAY

GROCERIES

FRIDAY	SATURDAY	SUNDAY	NOTES

GROCERIES

RECIPES

MONDAY	TUESDAY	WEDNESDAY	THURSDAY

GROCERIES

FRIDAY	SATURDAY	SUNDAY	NOTES

GROCERIES

RECIPES

MONDAY	TUESDAY	WEDNESDAY	THURSDAY

GROCERIES

FRIDAY	SATURDAY	SUNDAY	NOTES

GROCERIES

RECIPES

MONDAY	TUESDAY	WEDNESDAY	THURSDAY

GROCERIES

FRIDAY	SATURDAY	SUNDAY	NOTES

GROCERIES

RECIPES

MONDAY	TUESDAY	WEDNESDAY	THURSDAY

GROCERIES

FRIDAY	SATURDAY	SUNDAY	NOTES

GROCERIES

RECIPES

MONDAY	TUESDAY	WEDNESDAY	THURSDAY

FRIDAY	SATURDAY	SUNDAY	NOTES

MONDAY	TUESDAY	WEDNESDAY	THURSDAY

GROCERIES

FRIDAY	SATURDAY	SUNDAY	NOTES

GROCERIES

RECIPES

MONDAY	TUESDAY	WEDNESDAY	THURSDAY

GROCERIES

FRIDAY	SATURDAY	SUNDAY	NOTES

GROCERIES

RECIPES

MONDAY	TUESDAY	WEDNESDAY	THURSDAY

GROCERIES

FRIDAY	SATURDAY	SUNDAY	NOTES

GROCERIES

RECIPES

MONDAY	TUESDAY	WEDNESDAY	THURSDAY

GROCERIES

FRIDAY	SATURDAY	SUNDAY	NOTES

GROCERIES

RECIPES

<table>
<tr><th>MONDAY</th><th>TUESDAY</th><th>WEDNESDAY</th><th>THURSDAY</th></tr>
</table>

GROCERIES

<table>
<tr><th>FRIDAY</th><th>SATURDAY</th><th>SUNDAY</th><th>NOTES</th></tr>
</table>

GROCERIES

RECIPES

MONDAY	TUESDAY	WEDNESDAY	THURSDAY

GROCERIES

FRIDAY	SATURDAY	SUNDAY	NOTES

GROCERIES

RECIPES

<table>
<tr><th>MONDAY</th><th>TUESDAY</th><th>WEDNESDAY</th><th>THURSDAY</th></tr>
</table>

GROCERIES

<table>
<tr><th>FRIDAY</th><th>SATURDAY</th><th>SUNDAY</th><th>NOTES</th></tr>
</table>

GROCERIES

RECIPES

MONDAY	TUESDAY	WEDNESDAY	THURSDAY

GROCERIES

FRIDAY	SATURDAY	SUNDAY	NOTES

GROCERIES

RECIPES

<table>
<tr><td>MONDAY</td><td>TUESDAY</td><td>WEDNESDAY</td><td>THURSDAY</td></tr>
</table>

GROCERIES

<table>
<tr><td>FRIDAY</td><td>SATURDAY</td><td>SUNDAY</td><td>NOTES</td></tr>
</table>

GROCERIES

RECIPES

MONDAY	TUESDAY	WEDNESDAY	THURSDAY

GROCERIES

FRIDAY	SATURDAY	SUNDAY	NOTES

GROCERIES

RECIPES

www.ingramcontent.com/pod-product-compliance
Lightning Source LLC
Chambersburg PA
CBHW081310250726

48662CB00008B/2503